Fasting & Prayer Journal

A QUEENS GUIDE TO WINNING THROUGH
FASTING & PRAYER

Misty Goodwin

Misty Goodwin Enterprises LLC
P.O. Box 902
Milwaukee, Wisconsin 53201
https://coachmisty.org
misty@coachmisty.org
Access Life Classes at rockyourfavorcrown.com

Fasting & Prayer Journal Misty Goodwin —1st ed.

.

Proverbs 17:21

"But this kind does not go out except by prayer
and fasting."

My Testimony

I completed my first twenty-one day fast over eight years ago and that was the beginning of a new chapter that changed my life forever. I was in a very low place in my life and needed God to speak to me concerning my situation. When God challenged me to the fast, I was unfamiliar with preparing your mind, meals and prayers before starting a fast but I was crying out for help and desperate for change in my life. I obeyed God and by the fifteenth day, God showed up in a major way in my life.

I experienced major breakthrough and God turned my situation around without me having to experience back lash. Satan was a liar and God was exalted. God didn't answer my prayers the way that I thought he would, he did exceedingly, abundantly above all that I could ask or think.

It is my prayer that you will learn to develop a deeper intimate relationship with God, uncover anything and everything that is holding you back in life and experience major breakthroughs as you learn how to fast and pray.

-Coach Misty

ABC's Of Fasting

> ## 2 Chronicles 7:14
>
> *If my people, who are called by my name, will humble themselves and pray and seek my face and turn from their wicked ways, then I will hear from heaven, and I will forgive their sin and will heal their land.*

This guide will give you simple step by step instructions and devotionals to help you fast and pray effectively. There are many ways to fast and pray but I'm simply giving you the formula that has worked for me over eight years. Follow the formula and you will experience breakthrough. This is not a money back guarantee because it requires your actions, faith and persistence to go to work.

The word works when you work it. This is the way that I know how to get answers to unanswered questions, overcome spiritual warfare and discover the solutions to the problems that don't make sense. It doesn't matter if you've never fasted before or your'e ready to grow spiritually in your prayer life and your relationship with God. Expect to gain more knowledge and become effective in your spiritual growth and evolution.

Queens Slay The Enemy When You Fast & Pray

The A,B,C's Of Faith

Hebrews 11:1

Now faith is confidence in what we hope for and assurance about what we do not see.

The ABC's Of Faith is the simplest way to explain how to win the things that you desire by faith. The word NOW let's you know that what you're asking for is yours Now, you're just waiting on the manifestation.

Winning By Faith is just like a pageant, you declare that you've won before you participate. You prepare for the win, you believe in yourself and have confidence that you will walk away with the crown. The awesome thing about faith is the manifestation of your win will come to pass if you keep walking by faith and not by sight.

• Ask: Be specific about aiming your faith toward what you want or need from God. It's important that your faith has a target and be very specific about you're asking for. God loves you and he wants you

• Believe: Faith is believing in what you don't see. Your relationship with God is by faith. You may or may not have seen God but you believe he exists by faith. It's hard to explain but easy to believe because of something that you've experienced or encountered with God. He lives within you and his love for you is unfailing.

Doubt and unbelief will hinder your breakthrough while fasting and praying. Release your fears, worry, doubts and confusion.

Say It With Me:

Lord I Believe but help my unbelief.

Confess: Most people think that God knows what they need so they shouldn't have to ask. A child knows that their parents know when they are hungry or thirsty but they still ask. With that being said, ask for what you want and need because you're heavenly Father wants to give it to you.

Queen Etiquette: All Queens were born Winners

-Coach Misty

The ABC's Of Prayer

There are many ways to pray but I want to tach it in a simple structure so that anyone can grasp how to pray effectively. God desires for you to grow and mature in your prayers so he can use you to change the dynamics of your life as well as the life of others.

Prayer has three dimensions for you to reach and it requires you to live a righteous lifestyle to have access to heaven hearing you and God answering you.

The Outer Courts Of Prayer

The outer courts represents when you are saved yet still stuck in sin or your prayers evolve around asking God for things that he has already done, freeing you, things that are out of his will, deliverance, and protection. Usually your prayers are never answered because you pray amiss. You develop a belief that God doesn't answer your prayers but your issue is you don't know how to pray effectively.

Amiss-not quite right; inappropriate or out of place.

It's important for you to know that if you are sin, humble yourself and cry out to the Lord for help so your prayers are not hindered.

James 4:2-3 you desire but do not have, so you kill. You covet but you cannot get what you want, so you quarrel and fight. You do not have because you do not ask God. When you ask, you do not receive, because you ask with wrong motives, that you may spend what you get on your pleasures.

The Inner Courts Of Prayer

Praying from the Inner Courts is when you have come out of sin/selfishness and you begin to pray according to Gods will or his word. You learn to walk in authority and pray effectively where you see and witness results. You no longer just pray for yourself, you begin praying for others and desire to see God make changes in their lives. You see the manifestation of your prayers and experience breakthrough in your life as well as others.

When you live a life that is pleasing to God, he desires to answer your prayers and give you the desires of your heart.

James 5:16

Therefore confess your sins to each other and pray for each other so that you may be healed. The prayer of a righteous person is powerful and effective.

Prayers Answered From Heaven

Answered prayers from the third realm of heaven is the highest dimension of answered prayers that will manifest. This is where true Intercessors flow. In prayer, God will reveal to you the answer to the questions and give you the solutions to the problem. In this realm, God will also give you specific instructions on what to pray, who to pray for, a word of warning for others or yourself and expose you to the things that the enemy is secretly creating and give you a strategy for defeat. This is where God desires for all of his children to have access to so we can get the job done on earth.

1 Kings 8:30

Hear the supplication of your servant and of your people Israel when they pray toward this place. Hear from heaven, you're dwelling place, and when you hear, forgive.

1 John 5:14-16 14

This is the confidence we have in approaching God: that if we ask anything according to his will, he hears us. And if we know that he hears us—whatever we ask —we know that we have what we asked of him.

16If you see any brother or sister commit a sin that does not lead to death, you should pray and God will give them life. I refer to those whose sin does not lead to death. There is a sin that leads to death. I am not saying that you should pray about that.

Fast Prep

Before you begin your fast, prepare to go to the store and buy the right foods. Plan out your meals before you get started and pack a lunch everyday for work or school so you won't use that as an excuse to fall.

Fasting can become just dieting without you eating, praying and meditating to hear Gods answer. You must be disciplined and desire to experience breakthrough through fasting and prayer. Food prep is life or death to your fast. I will give you some recommendations. See a doctor if you are sick or taking medication before participating in a fast.

These are my recommendations but use wisdom and judgement to discern where you are physically. Fasting is a supernatural experience. As you push back your plate and die to your flesh, you become sensitive to the spirit as God speaks to you concerning your requests and petitions.

Fasting requires you to push back your plate and sacrifice to experience the supernatural experience in Gods presence. This journal and devotional was created for a 21 day fast but you can choose how many days that you will fast. Every year I do a corporate fast with Rock Your Favor Crown Movement. You can go there and hear the 21 daily devotions and prayer for this book for free at rockyourfavorcrown.com

Things To Give Up For The Fast

Coffee, Soda, Energy Drinks, alcohol, sugar/foods that contain sugar, all meat & sex.

What You Can Have For The Fast

Fruit, Vegetables, Broth, Natural Juice, Nuts, Oatmeal & Grains, Tea, Water, Seafood, Smoothies, Protein Shakes, Eggs, Bread, Crackers, Cheese, Peanut Butter, Milk of any sort.

1 Corinthians 7:4-5

The wife does not have authority over her own body but yields it to her husband. In the same way, the husband does not have authority over his own body but yields it to his wife. 5Do not deprive each other except perhaps by mutual consent and for a time, so that you may devote yourselves to prayer. Then come together again so that Satan will not tempt you because of your lack of self-control.

Beginners:

If you've never fasted before, start with giving up one type of food that you love for the full 21 days. This could be caffeine, meat, fast food etc.

If you have health conditions that require you to eat, sacrifice TV, radio etc.

Intermediate:

No food from 6am-12pm.

Only smoothies, natural juice, tea, water, protein shakes.

12pm-5:55am eat whatever you want.

Advanced:

No food from 6am-12pm.

Only smoothies, natural juice, tea, water, protein shakes.

12pm-5:55am

Fruit, Vegetables, Natural Juice, Nuts, Oatmeal & Grains, Tea, Water, Seafood, Smoothies, Protein Shakes, Eggs, Bread, Crackers, Cheese, Peanut Butter, Beans, Rice, Milk of any sort.

Food Prep

If you prepare your food ahead of time it will be easier to maintain your fast.

Go to the store ahead of time and buy everything you need.

Food Prep Ideas

Protein shakes or smoothies are filling if you drink them as a meal replacement in the morning.

Soup/Vegetable Chili-Make a pot of soup or chili, separate it in containers and freeze it so you can have it on days you may be weak.

Salmon-Quick and easy to prepare grilled or baked in oven.

Crab Legs/Shrimp-Add boil seasoning and water and they are ready in 20 minutes.

Beans and Rice-Prepare ahead of time, separate into containers and freeze it until you need it.

Salad-Boil your eggs ahead of time so you can add them to a salad or eat them alone for protein.

Mind Prep

Philippians 4:8

Finally, brothers and sisters, whatever is true, whatever is noble, whatever is right, whatever is pure, whatever is lovely, whatever is admirable--if anything is excellent or praiseworthy--think about such things.

You have to prepare your mind for the warfare that will fight your flesh as you discipline your body. Resisting foods that you desire will be challenging. Your plans to experience breakthrough will require you to defeat the lies that Satan will tell you as you go through these 21 Days.

- Keep your thoughts on good things and good reports.

- Desire the truth because the truth shall set you free.

- Think about the faithfulness of God and you will eventually experience it in your life.

- Pure thoughts will deliver you from lust and it's desires.

- Think about how lovely things will overtake your life.

- Think about the excellent things that God is doing in your life.

- Praise is your weapon for breakthrough in your life.

- Die to your flesh daily, denying yourself is the sacrifice.

Regulate your mind to think on good things and good reports so you can see and experience what your heart desires. You will defeat the enemy by regulating your mind on a daily basis. God wants you to experience his best because you are his Queen and he has promises that no man can take from you. Trust God for everything that your heart desires and go through this journey expecting you're Heavenly Father to perform miracles, signs and wonders in your life.

Set your mind everyday simply means resetting anything in your thoughts that are impure, defiled and carry contamination that will hinder you from walking by faith. Expect the enemy to play mind games with you about eating what you desire, having lustful thoughts, feeling weak in your body, nausea and being light headed. You have to keep telling yourself that YOU CAN DO ALL THINGS THROUGH CHRIST WHO STRENGTHENS YOU. In your weakness, God is made strong. All he requires for you is to ask him to strengthen you in your weak moments.

Prayer Barriers

Prayer barriers are obstacles that prevent the manifestation of your answered prayers. There are a few things that stand in the way of you receiving your breakthrough so let's discuss them.

Isaiah 58:4 What good is fasting when you keep on fighting and quarreling? This kind of fasting will never get you anywhere with me.

Keep your heart clear of any drama, confusion or cussing. Fasting creates a sacred atmosphere between you and God. The warfare and drama will be created to distract you from getting in Gods presence. Avoid any foolishness at all costs and be the peacemaker at all times so that you can experience breakthrough.

Guard your ears, eyes and heart from opening the door to any drama that will be used to hinder l you, whatever you ask for in prayer, believe that you have received it, and it will be yours. And when you stand praying, if you hold anything against anyone, forgive them, so that your Father in heaven may forgive you your sins." You have to believe that God is a rewarder of those who seek him. You are a Daughter of Royalty, a Queen in the Kingdom so come to God as his child so he can prosper your life.

Mark 11:23-25

Truly If I tell you, if anyone says to this mountain, 'Go, throw yourself into the sea,' and does not doubt in their heart but believes that what they say will happen, it will be done for them. Therefore I tell you, whatever you ask for in prayer, believe that you have received it, and it will be yours. And when you stand praying, if you hold anything against anyone, forgive them, so that your Father in heaven may forgive you your sins."

Un-forgiveness is a major barricade to block your breakthrough in fasting and prayer. Before you stand praying, forgive any and everyone so your prayers are not hindered.

1 Peter 3:7

Husbands, in the same way, treat your wives with consideration as a delicate vessel, and with honor as fellow heirs of the gracious gift of life, so that your prayers will not be hindered.

It's important that if your'e married, that you and your husband keep a clear heart so your prayers are never hindered.

Hebrews 11:6

And without faith it is impossible to please God, because anyone who comes to him must believe that he exists and that he rewards those who earnestly seek him.

Unbelief will hinder, distract and detour you from experiencing the manifestation of miracles, signs and wonders during a fast. You must have an expectation that God will answer your prayers. Your faith will manifest the answer.

Isaiah 59:2

But your iniquities have made a separation between you and your God, And your sins have hidden His face from you so that He does not hear.

Sin will block you from having an encounter from God. Be Holy for God is holy. You have to treat your body as a temple so you must honor and respect your relationship with God. Do everything in your power to turn away from sin and walk in self control.

James 4:7

Submit yourselves, then, to God. Resist the devil, and he will flee from you.

A Fasted Lifestyle

Therefore, I urge you, brothers and sisters, in view of God's mercy, to offer your bodies as a living sacrifice, holy and pleasing to God—this is your reasonable service.

God would rather you live a fasted lifestyle instead of fasting for a few days and going back into sin. A fasted lifestyle is when you present your body as a living sacrifice and submit to Gods perfect will for your life. If you live according to Gods will and honor your body as Gods temple, you will see God answering your prayers daily, hear Gods voice clearly and stay in the perfect will of God.

Satan loves when you fast only once a year and live a lifestyle of sin, fear or rebellion. He knows that he controls your life when your'e not submitted to God and God only has your attention for 21 days or however many days that you fast. God desires for you to raise the standard of his Kingdom and arise as a Queen by living a fasted lifestyle. We understand that God showed us the benefits of fasting and prayer throughout the bible and desires for us to fast for the right reasons.

Whenever we seek God for his perfect will and live by his principles, he will honor any sacrifice that you give. Living a righteous and fasted lifestyle gives you access to receiving anything we ask God for because your desires become what God desires for you.

Gods Promises For Righteous Living

- John 15:7 Ask Him Anything

- 1 John 5:14-16 He Hears You

- Proverbs 37:3-5 Desires Of Your Heart Granted

- Mark 11:23-25 Mountains Removed

- Psalms 1:1-5 You Will Prosper

- Psalms 112 Wealth & Riches

- James 5:16 Your Prayers Availeth Much

- Matthew 6:33 Things Will Be Added To You

- Jeremiah 33:3 God Will Show You The Things To Come

- Matthew 7:7-8 Ask & It Shall Be Given

- Psalms 62:8 Make Your Requests

All of the promises of God are yes and amen

Prayers That Manifest The Answer

2 Chronicles 7:14

If my people, who are called by my name, will humble themselves and pray and seek my face and turn from their wicked ways, then I will hear from heaven, and I will forgive their sin and will heal their land.

I will never forget the feeling I had of God not wanting to answer my prayers. When I was learning to pray, my prayers were generic and I wasn't sure if God heard me. I stuck to praying everyday as the Holy Spirit assisted me on how to effectively get my prayers answered. As my prayer life matured, I desired to teach others how to pray and get an answer from God.

God is forever answering prayers but I learned that if I came to God and strategized my requests, I would see the answer manifested. If you follow these guidelines, I know that you will experience breakthrough as you fast and pray.

The Posture Of Prayer:

- Desire to seek God through fasting & prayer Isaiah 55:6

- Return to the Lord with all of your heart. Joel 2:12

- Humble Yourself before God and acknowledge that he is the head of your life. 1 Peter 5:6

- Seek Gods face to develop a more intimate relationship with God. Daniel 9:3-4

- Repent of your sins known and unknown. 1 Peter 1:14-15

- Forgive others of their transgressions Mark 11:23-25

- Enter into his gates with thanksgiving & enter into his courts with praise. This is an important part of prayer, if you start prayer by thanking God for who he is and not for what your'e asking him for. This opens up your heart and ears to hear God speak to you. Get excited about the conversation you will have with God about your situation. He desires to send angels on assignment to give you the answer to your prayers. Psalms 84:1-12

- Be anxious for nothing as you go into prayer, you can't rush God in prayer. Rest in knowing that God wants you to know the answer and he doesn't want you rushing him to give you clarity or the answer. Prayer develops your communication with God but you must trust him to have your best interests at hand. Philippians 4:6

- Make your requests to God with an expectation that God is going to give you what you ask. God knows what you need but you still have to ask him. It's just like a child that is hungry, a child knows that their parents know when they need to feed them but they still say they are hungry.

- God hears you when you pray and he is going to answer you. Hearing the answer requires you to set the atmosphere of worship and meditate as he downloads the answer from heaven. The answer will be clear and precise and you won't be confused if you listen and obey his voice. 1 John 5:14-15

- Keep Asking, Keep Seeking, Keep Knocking, all answers will not be given on the 1st day of your fast or when you pray. Be persistent in your pursuit and watch God manifest the answer to your prayers Matthew 7:7-8

- Have faith in the promises of God that he hears your prayers and will answer you. God is a rewarder of those who diligently seek him. You are WINNING BY FAITH!

Dear Lord,

I thank you for being so awesome in my life. I ask that you forgive me of my sins known and unknown. As I begin this 21 day fast, I ask that you strengthen my natural abilities to resist my fleshly desires and any side effects that I may experience through food addictions. Teach me to walk in self control as I seek your perfect will for my life. Thank you in advance for giving me the answer to my questions and the solutions to my problems. I will fight the good fight of faith and in my weakness you will be my strength. I will have the victory through fasting and prayer. In Jesus Name Amen

The Benefits Of Fasting

Fasting will teach you to die to your flesh, walk in the spirit & help you to remove the lust that encourages you to do what your flesh desires. It teaches you to develop self control and spiritual discipline. It exposes the hidden agenda of Satan and his wicked devices that he uses to control you.

Fasting makes it easier to be quiet and allow God to fight the enemy on your behalf, he will unveil the struggles that you have that has held you back and take the handcuffs off of you.

* Spiritual Growth & Maturity

* The habits that create self control that are essential for your victory.

* The pulling down of strongholds

* Destroy Generational Curses

* Sever Soul Ties

* Become sensitive to the voice of God

8 Things to expect as you fast & pray.

- Breakthrough

- Wisdom & Clarity

- Guidance & Direction

- Deliverance

- Restoration

- Vindication

- The answers to your questions

- Healing

Give God Back Your Crown

Isaiah 62:3

You will be a crown of splendor in the Lord's hand,

A royal diadem in the hand of your God.

As Queens we can easily allow pride and rebellion creep into our lives by doing things according to the world versus doing things according to Gods word. As a Queen our role comes with a great responsibility to live according to our core values and Kingdom principles. It's easy to drift away from the standard God gave us in order to attain the things our flesh desires instead of desiring to live to please God.

Queen Vashti is a great example of a Queen that allowed the spirit of pride, selfishness and rebellion to disqualify her from being Queen. The awesome thing about us is we can return to God, repent and get back in right standing with him. It's important for us to answer when the King calls us to live as Kingdom Women, Kingdom Wives & Kingdom Families.

The focus of this fast is to place our crowns back in Gods hands so he can polish us in order for us to become wiser mothers, wives, leaders, influencers and servants. As I was in prayer for this years focus for the fast, I saw God take our crowns in a vision and begin to polish them up until they shined so bright that I needed glasses to look at them. After God finished shining our crowns up, he placed them back on our heads and affirmed our positions and assignments in his Kingdom. God said to me that when we completed this fast, we would see and experience Victory, Breakthrough and Favor with God and Man.

The crown represents our position in the Royal Family, Our Authority, Our Influence, Gods Favor, Gods Light that should shine & the representation of a WINNER. As you complete this fast you will win at faith, family, finances, love, marriage, your future and attain Favor from God.

For the next 21 days set aside 15-30 minutes a day to spend in the presence of God. You can do this early in the morning, on your lunch break or late at night. Expect God to create miracles, signs and wonders as you experience a greater, intimate relationship with God.

Be it unto you according to your Faith, nobody can hinder your breakthrough but you. Have faith in God that he will do exceedingly, abundantly, above all that you can ask or think. Ignore the naysayer and those who don't believe in fasting and prayer. By the end of this fast, single Queens will discover hidden struggles that has held you back from being a wife and married Queens will uncover the hidden struggles that have hindered their marriage.

Luke 1:45 Blessed is she who has believed that the Lord would fulfill his promises to her!"

Day 1

Pleasing Your Husband

Living a life to please your husband is required to stay in the perfect will of God. If you are single, God is your husband and will promote you to be a Wife when you are ready. Pleasing God teaches you how to please your husband.

Meditation:

1 Corinthians 7:34 An unmarried woman or virgin is concerned about the Lord's affairs: Her aim is to be devoted to the Lord in both body and spirit. But a married woman is concerned about the affairs of this world--how she can please her husband.

Examination:

Single: How are you focused on serving God? Serving God is teaching you to be a Helpmeet so start serving God with your Gifts, Talents, Time & Money.

Married: Are you doing everything in your power to please your husband? What is he asking of you that you're not giving? What can you do differently to ensure that you please your husband?

Show more affection
Spend more time with him
Do more around the house on weekends

Single Wife Prayer:

Dear Lord,

Teach me to live a life that is pleasing in your sight. Forgive me for having a desire to please a man more than I desire to please you. I desire to be a Helpmeet to you so you can teach me to become the Helpmeet for my husband. I will refocus by preparing to be a Wife vs. thirsting for a man thats not my husband.

In Jesus Name Amen

Wife Prayer:

Dear Lord,

My desire is to please my husband on a daily basis. Help me to see and discern his needs and wants and be willing to give them to him. Any voids of emptiness that I feel I'm not getting, speak to my husband to help him to meet my needs. Let us both have a desire to please one another. Anything that has held us back from doing that, expose, reveal and remove it.

In Jesus Name Amen

Make Your Request:

_____

_____

_____

_____

Notes:

_____

_____

_____

_____

_____

_____

_____

Day 2

Cherish Your Vows

In a marriage you must cherish your vows that you made to God. If you are single, it's important for you to keep the vows that you made to God to live holy, present your body to God as a living sacrifice and serve God and remain faithful to him to prove that you are wife material. If you are married, you must cherish the vows you made to God, your husband and yourself. If you focus on being faithful to your role, God will teach your husband to be faithful to his.

Meditation:
Ecclesiastes 5:5 It is better not to make a vow than to make one and not fulfill it.

Examination:
Examine yourself to see if you are keeping your Vows(commitments & promises) to God/in your marriage.

Single: What have you made to God that you have not kept? What will you do differently to keep your Vows?

_____

_____

_____

_____

_____

_____

_____

Married: What Vows have you not kept? What will you do differently to keep your Vows?

_____

_____

_____

_____

_____

_____

Single Wife Prayer:

Dear Lord,

Forgive me for not keeping my vows , promises & commitments. I repent for not recognizing the importance of this season of my life, as you teach me how to be a Kingdom Wife. I understand that my husband can't find me until I'm ready, so I choose to be a Wife for Christ so I can be committed to my husband.

In Jesus Name Amen

Wife Prayer:

Dear Lord,

I understand that when I said my Vows, I not only made a Vow to my husband but most importantly to you. My marriage is a Holy Matrimony and I will not allow any person, place or thing to stand in the way of our marriage. Help me in the areas of my weaknesses and strengthen me to never give up. What you have put together, let no man separate.

In Jesus Name Amen

Make Your Request:

_____

_____

_____

_____

_____

_____

Notes:

_____

_____

_____

_____

_____

_____

_____

_____

Day 3

Polish Your Crown

As you place your crown in Gods hands, he will reveal to you the areas that have been dimmed because of your character flaws. God has Queen Etiquette which means to be a doer of his word. Un-forgiveness, bitterness, resentment, rejection, pride, selfishness, lack of knowledge and sin dims your light where God wants you to shine. Gold is refined in the fire where it burns off the impurities that will hinder the purity, quality and the value of the gold. Up-grade your value as a Queen and a wife by getting rid of the quality flaws that dim your shine.

Meditation:
Proverbs 12:4
An excellent wife is the crown of her husband, But she who shames him is like rottenness in his bones.

Examination:

Single:
What are some things that dim the Shine Of Your Crown & brings God shame?

_____

_____

_____

_____

_____

_____

_____

_____

Married:

What are some things that dim the Shine Of Your Crown & brings your husband shame?

What did God reveal to you in prayer in order to help you change your behavior?

_____

_____

_____

_____

_____

_____

_____

Single Wife Prayer:

Dear Lord,
Forgive me for bringing you shame. Help me to prepare to be an excellent Wife. I'm yielded to be faithful to you so you can teach me to become a winning wife that glorifies you. Create in me a clean heart and renew a right spirit within me. Help me to desire what you desire for me as I keep my heart pure before you.
In Jesus Name Amen

Wife Prayer:

Dear Lord,
Forgive me for bringing you shame by not fulfilling my assignment as a Kingdom Wife. Expose, reveal and remove any habits, dysfunctional behavior, emotional distress or attitude that causes my Crown to become dull. Create in me a clean heart and renew a right spirit within me. Teach me to become an excellent Wife so my Crown Can Bling for your glory.
In Jesus Name Amen

Heart Examination:

_____

_____

_____

_____

_____

_____

Day 4

Your Crown Should Have Gems

Meditation:

Isaiah 45:3 And I will give you treasures hidden in the darkness-secret riches. I will do this so you may know that I am the LORD, the God of Israel, the one who calls you by name.

Examination: You must be tried in the fire for your gold & dig for your Gems to make your Crown Bling. These materials are manifested through your relationship pains, frustrations & struggles. You have to dig deep within & search for growth, maturity & breakthrough. As you pass the faith tests, God applies more Gold & places more Gems on your crown.

Single: Stop being a Girlfriend & Become A Bride For Christ. Holy, Trustworthy, Submitted & Faithful To God. What area do you need to work on?

_____

_____

_____

_____

_____

_____

The Fire is burning off your past & severing the soul ties from your Exes so you can receive a pure heart of gold that's not tainted by your past. The cuts of life is what will allow your Gems to shine for Gods glory. Embrace this process and never give up on God perfecting you.

Wife: The warfare as well as the things that frustrate & irritate you in marriage will put you in the fire so you can be a pure, authentic Kingdom Wife. Where are you being burned?

_____

_____

_____

_____

_____

_____

Don't resist the process because everything that you're going through in your marriage is placing Gems on your Crown To Bling.

Single Wife Prayer:

Dear Lord,
Help me to stay in the fire until everything that's not like you burns off of me. Teach me to walk in Self Control so I don't give up on my Process To becoming a Wife.
In Jesus Name Amen

Wife Prayer:

Dear Lord,
I thank you for refining me in the fire to burn off anything/everything that is hindering me from being the wife that I need to be. I thank you for allowing the heat to expose, reveal and remove anything in my husband that's attempting to hurt our marriage.
In Jesus Name Amen

Desires For Your Husband:

_____

_____

_____

_____

_____

Make Your Request:

_____

_____

_____

_____

_____

Notes:

_____

_____

_____

_____

_____

_____

_____

Day 5

Die To Your Flesh

Your flesh is a mess and you can't win a fight by faith when your'e fighting from the fleshly realm. You are dealing with darkness, wickedness and Satan using everything in his power to kill, steal and destroy you and your marriage. He doesn't want Kingdom marriages to advance because he knows that two are better than one. If you fight in the flesh, it will be a bloody mess. Fight in the spirit and you will resist fighting in the flesh.

Meditation:
Mark 10:8 and the two will become one flesh.' So they are no longer two, but one flesh.

Examination:
In order for you to become one with God or your husband, it requires you to die to your flesh. The Holy Spirit will become your comforter & mediator as you let no flesh dwell among you. You will then be able to walk in the spirit, develop self control and overcome your struggles.

Single:
What are some fleshly desires that is hindering you from becoming one with God?

_____

_____

_____

_____

_____

_____

Wife:
What fleshly things hinder you from becoming one with your husband?

_____

_____

_____

_____

_____

_____

Ephesians 6:12 or our struggle is not against flesh and blood, but against the rulers, against the authorities, against the powers of this dark world and against the spiritual forces of evil in the heavenly realms.

Single Wife Prayer:
Dear Lord,
Help me to die to my fleshly desires. Expose & uproot anything in me that is hindering me from becoming the Kingdom Wife you've chosen me to be.
In Jesus Name Amen

Wife Prayer:
Dear Lord,
Thank you for helping me to be one with my husband. Help me to die to my flesh and become one with the Holy Spirit so I can see and experience breakthrough in my marriage.
In Jesus Name Amen

Husband Desires:

_____

_____

_____

_____

_____

_____

_____

_____

Day 6

Are You Teachable?

As much as you believe that you have it all together, you must remain humble and position yourself as a student so the Holy Spirit can teach you to evolve into the winning wife, servant, mother, influencer and Queen that you are. Get wisdom and get understanding from those that are teaching according to Gods word and not the standards of this world.

Meditation:
1 John 2:27 But the anointing that you received from him abides in you, and you have no need that anyone should teach you. But as his anointing teaches you about everything, and is true, and is no lie—just as it has taught you, abide in him.

Examination:
The Holy Spirit is your teacher. He is preparing you to be a Wife or equipping you to win in your marriage.

There are things that you don't know that the Holy Spirit will reveal to you. Its up to you to hear, listen & obey. The Holy Spirit will always lead you to the truth that sets you free from hidden lies. You have to discern what to do with the information that he is leading you to because the truth will set you free.

Wife Prayer-Single Or Married:

Dear Lord,
Thank you for giving me the Holy Spirit that is teaching me to be a Kingdom Wife. Lead, guide & direct me to the right people, places & things that will give me the wise counsel & guidance to Win At Love & marriage.

I embrace my evolution to become a Kingdom Wife. I will remain teachable and do what the word, the Holy Spirit & wise counsel tells me to do. If I have any resistance, pride, lack of knowledge, independence, strongholds or generational curses that are hindering me, reveal it to me and give me the wisdom that I need to make the necessary changes in my life.
In Jesus Name Amen

Areas That You Need Wisdom:

_____

_____

_____

_____

_____

_____

_____

_____

Make Your Request:

_____

_____

_____

_____

_____

_____

Notes:

_____

_____

_____

_____

_____

_____

_____

_____

Day 7

The Evolution Of A Kingdom Wife

Never feel comfortable about where you are in your spiritual growth maturity that helps you to evolve in every area of your life. The enemy wants you to stay stuck at the same place you are year after year spiritually. God desires for you to go from faith to faith and glory to glory. We all have room to grow up in our relationship with God as well as in our marriage.

Your mentality about where you are will hinder, distract and detour you if you were raised in a dysfunctional home or are content with where you are in your marriage. God desires for you to grow and mature in wisdom, knowledge and understanding for every area of your life. You must desire to grow so Gods favor can overtake you and your family.

Meditation:
Luke 2:52 And Jesus grew in wisdom and stature, and in favor with God and man.

Examination:

In order to evolve as a Wife, you're required to grow spiritually and become wiser than you were. Every level of spiritual promotion requires a higher version of yourself.

Singles: What area of your life do you need wisdom as it relates to preparing to be a Wife, Love & Marriage?

_____

_____

_____

_____

_____

_____

_____

Wives: What area of your marriage do you need to become a wiser wife? This will be the area that you struggle the most in your marriage.

_____

_____

_____

Single Wife Prayer:

Dear Lord,

I desire to grow and evolve into being a Kingdom Wife. Lead, guide and direct me in the areas that I struggle and prepare me to be a Winning Wife. Tear down any pride in me that will destroy me.

In Jesus Name Amen

Wife Prayer:

Dear Lord,

You know the areas that I struggle & fall short as a Wife. I desire to grow, evolve and mature into a Winning Wife that my crown will shine for your glory. Tear down any pride in me that will destroy me.

In Jesus Name Amen

Wisdom Nuggets:

_____

_____

_____

_____

_____

_____

_____

Day 8

A Wise Woman Builds Her House

A wise woman builds her life, family and marriage with the word of God. It's foolish of you to do life without Gods word. It's foolish of you to desire love without desiring God. It's foolish for you to tear down your husband, marriage or family by speaking death instead of life over every situation and circumstance.

The enemy loves women who don't walk in authority as a Queen in the Kingdom of God. You have authority over sickness, dysfunction, confusion, foolishness, infidelity, financial struggles, a rebellious child and the list goes on. You can decree a thing and it shall be established and the light shall shine on your ways. The things that you can't change, you can speak a word and the earth must listen to you. Choose to speak life and live by the word, that is what builds your house. Take the bricks that the enemy throws to block you and build your life in abundance.

Meditation:
Proverbs 14:1 The wise woman builds her house, but with her own hands the foolish one tears hers down.

Examination:
There are materials that you use that can tear down your sanctuary(your home). Your words, attitude issues,

withholding sex(Wives only) negative disposition, dysfunctional behavior, independence & lack of knowledge. Not prioritizing by putting 1st things 1st, jealousy, envy, strife. This is the behavior of a foolish woman.

Singles:
You should be building your life on The foundation of Gods Word. Your focus should be in building your relationship with God, Your credit, your self esteem, your relationship with your children.

What areas of your life are torn down that needs to be restored?

_____

_____

_____

_____

_____

_____

_____

Wives:
You should be building your marriage on the foundation of Gods Word. Marriage takes two people to fully invest in pleasing each other. When you place the focus on you, the materials of me, myself & I will tear down your man & your marriage.

You may have some requests & legitimate concerns to repair your sanctuary but seek God On how to approach your needs & concerns.

What are ways that you tear down your man & your marriage?

_____

_____

_____

_____

_____

_____

_____

Rebuild Your Self Esteem:

_____

_____

_____

_____

_____

_____

_____

Single Wife Prayer:

Dear Lord,

Forgive me for tearing down what you've built up in my life. Show me the areas of my life that need to be repaired or restored in my life so I won't be my own hindrance from receiving my husband. I need you to help me.

In Jesus Name Amen

Wife Prayer:

Dear Lord,

Forgive me for tearing down my man & my marriage. Help me to be the Kingdom Wife that you've called me to be. Help me to repair & restore the areas of my marriage that have been torn down so you can get the glory in my marriage.

In Jesus Name Amen

Ways You Will Build Your Husband Up:

_____

_____

_____

_____

_____

_____

_____

Make Your Request:

_____

_____

_____

_____

_____

Notes:

_____

_____

_____

_____

_____

_____

_____

Day 9

Deliverance From Sexual Frustration

Meditation:
Hebrews 13:4 Marriage should be honored by all, and the marriage bed kept pure, for God will judge the adulterer and all the sexually immoral.

Examination:
The Enemy will use anything to defile the marriage bed. As a Wife rather you are Single or Married, you must conduct yourself in a way that you leave no room for the devil.
The lust of the eyes, pornography, masturbation or your deceitful heart will defile your marriage bed.

Single:
You need to be celibate for the right reasons. Guard your heart, mind, body & soul from any lustful desires that will cause you to fall. Be Holy for God is Holy

What is your weakness from falling prey to defiling your marriage bed?

Sex before marriage usually leads to divorce. During your season of being alone, God teaches you how to die to your flesh and walk in self control.

Soul ties entangle you in a memory or experience with your X so that you never enjoy your Y. This is why you need to purge from your past so you can enjoy your future.

When you do it Gods way, once you get married you will be able to sustain your marriage through the self control you learned when you were single.

Wives: The biggest issue that husbands have with their wives is when women withhold sex when they are mad or use sex to manipulate their husbands in order to get their way.
You both must agree on fulfilling each other's sexual needs. Your body is not your own. Don't go to bed angry, mad or bitter, make peace and remain intimate with your husband. Leave no room for the devil.

Another issue is when you never get over your X and desire for your husband to meet the needs from the marks another man left on your soul. Trying to repeat that sensation or position will leave your soul thirsting for old satisfaction. This can be an issue for your husband as well and needs to be covered in the blood of Jesus and uprooted.

If you've never been delivered from soul ties, this can create sexual frustration in your marriage. You must teach each other how to please one another by being open about your needs & desires.

Another issue that brings sexual frustration is if you've been molested, raped or sexually abused and there are things that remind you of what happened to you by touch or position. It's challenging for your husband to know what your struggles are if you don't communicate them to him.

Most men are sensitive to your past experiences and will be willing to walk out you're healing together. Give your husband the opportunity to help you with what you're suffering through privately. Honest communication will destroy the lies of Satan in your bedroom.

Finally Leave no room for the devil in your bedroom.

Struggles Of Sexual Frustration:

_____

_____

_____

_____

_____

_____

_____

_____

_____

_____

_____

_____

Single Wife Prayer:
Dear Lord,
Forgive me for defiling my bedroom before marriage. I desire to live a lifestyle of purification & remain celibate until I marry. Help me to treat my body as your temple. Sever any soul ties, strongholds or generational curses in our life. Thank you for helping me to remain kept and hidden until my husband finds me. In Jesus Name Amen

Wife Prayer:
Dear Lord,
Forgive me if I have lusted in any way toward anyone other than my husband. Anything that I have done to defile my covenant or any thoughts that would defile my marriage bedroom, free my husband and I from captivity. Help my husband and I to desire to please one another and satisfy each other's needs so we never leave room for the enemy.
In Jesus Name Amen

Healing From Infidelity:

_____

_____

_____

_____

_____

_____

Day 10

Your Body Is Your Temple

God desires for you to prosper in all that you do. He is concerned about your health mentally, physically, emotionally and spiritually. It's important for you to take care of you because after all that you do for others, it means nothing if you have neglected yourself. You need to learn to eat to live by putting the right foods in your body. The wrong foods are traced to sickness and disease.

Isaiah 53:5 But he was pierced for our transgressions, he was crushed for our iniquities; the punishment that brought us peace was on him, and by his stripes we are healed.

You should go to the doctor for you're yearly exams. If you are dealing with an illness, know that Jesus paid the price for you're healing and all you have to do is receive it.

If you are suffering from any mental illness, don't be ashamed to ask for help. Go to counseling, hire a therapist or psychologist and don't apologize for getting what you need in life.

Deal with your emotional distress, anxiety, stress, worry, fear and doubt. All of these symptoms are rooted in not trusting God for your life. This can be destroyed by developing a stronger relationship with God and through fasting/prayer.

Meditation:

3 John 2 Beloved, I wish above all things that thou mayest prosper and be in health, even as thy soul prospers.

Examination:

In order to experience health & wellness in your body, you must treat your body like your temple. This includes a stress free, worry free, healthy balance.

Gluttony is a sin and an open door to sickness and disease. You have to eat to live by not contaminating your body with foods that carry & manifest sickness.

Do you get 6-8 hours of rest daily?
Do you live to eat or eat To Live?
Do you worry and stress about things you can't control?
Do you workout at least 3 times a week with cardio?

What areas do you struggle in treating your body as the temple of the Holy Spirit?

_____

_____

_____

_____

_____

_____

_____

_____

_____

_____

_____

_____

_____

_____

Prayer For Singles & Wives:

Dear Lord,

Forgive me if I've defiled my temple in any way. Cleanse, purge & purify me in the blood of Jesus. Help me to eat healthier, exercise and take better care of myself. I cast my cares upon you and rest in knowing that you will take care of any worry, doubt, fear or stress in my life. I choose to live life in wholeness of Mind, Body & Soul. I am delivered from everything that the enemy had me bound to
In Jesus Name Amen

Make Your Request:

_____

_____

_____

_____

_____

_____

Notes:

_____

_____

_____

_____

_____

_____

_____

Day 11

Guard Your Heart

Guarding your heart is simply putting your head in the game. Your heart is deceitful but your head is developed through the mind of Christ. Your life is transformed by renewing your mind to Gods word. Let your head guard your heart & you won't be deceived.

Ask God for discernment to make wise decisions and choose those around you wisely so you don't allow your heart to misguide you.

Meditation:
Proverbs 4:23 Above all else, guard your heart, for everything you do flows from it.

Examination:
The issues of life will clog your heart from receiving the love you deserve or giving the love that is needed. If you get caught up in Un-forgiveness, bitterness, resentment or rejection. Being deceived by false love can be blocked by seeking God to ask him to reveal the motives that people have toward you. Don't become false love because of the

painful situations life has thrown you. Live through it, grow from it and move on.

Single/Wife:

What issues in your life has created a wall that is blocking your heart from giving or receiving love? How does your heart deceive you? How are you deceived by cubic zirconia love versus genuine love?

_____

_____

_____

_____

_____

_____

_____

_____

_____

_____

_____

_____

_____

Single & Married Wife Prayer:
Dear Lord,
Teach me to guard my heart from the issues of my life. I release any in-forgiveness, resentment or bitterness. Give me discernment to make wise decisions & choose those around me wisely. Create in me a clean heart and renew a right spirit within me. I desire to have pure heart that loves freely. Teach me to love like you and freely forgive those who despitefully uses me.
In Jesus Name Amen

Do A Heart Examination:

_____

_____

_____

_____

_____

_____

_____

_____

_____

_____

Day 12

Teach Me How To Love

Gods love covers a multitude of sins. The first thing that love requires is patience. You must put love in its proper place for it to sustain your relationships. Love God, love yourself & you will discover how to love others.

Meditation:

Mark 12:30-31 Love the Lord your God with all your heart and with all your soul and with all your mind and with all your strength.' The second is this: 'Love your neighbor as yourself.' There is no commandment greater than these."

Examination:

It's easy to love when things are going right. The challenge is loving other's when things are going wrong. Marriage requires two imperfect people to love one another through Gods perfection.

Wives: False expectations, disappointment, frustration, impatience, hurt, shame, guilt & becoming weary while waiting for change to take place in your marriage can challenge you to love your spouse through their transformation.

Singles:

Don't awaken love until your'e ready. Your season of being alone is preparing you to become suitable for your husband. During this season of your life, it's important that you develop an intimate relationship with God. Experience Self Love By loving yourself enough to say no to people who don't value you. What area do you Struggle with love?

_____

_____

_____

_____

_____

_____

_____

Wives:

Examine your love and discover the areas that you fall short of loving your husband through your imperfections.

_____

_____

_____

_____

_____

_____

_____

Single Wife Prayer:
Dear Lord,
Teach me to love like you. Give me patience to wait on you're timing as you prepare me for my King. Forgive me for desiring a man more than I desire you. Help me to stay focused on submitting to you as you lead me to walk in your perfect will.
In Jesus Name Amen

Wife Prayer:
Dear Lord,
Help me to love my husband with your unconditional love. Teach me to cover his weaknesses in prayer and see him through your eyes. What you have put together, let no man separate us. Our love will continue to grow and flow together through your perfection and we will embrace the process that is teaching us to love like you.
In Jesus Name Amen

Day 13

Jesus Cover Girl Model

Meditation:

1 Peter 4:8 Above all, love each other deeply, because love covers over a multitude of sins.

Examination:

God created woman from flesh and bone of a man. The purpose of the rib is to cover the flesh, protect the heart & assist the lungs to breathe properly. Our roles as wives is to cover our husbands flesh. When you said I do, you said I do to dealing with his struggles & shortcomings.

Love covers a multitude of sins. This doesn't excuse his behavior. You will defeat his struggles through Fasting & Prayer. Until you get married, you must learn how to die to your flesh daily. Coming into a marriage with lust & flesh struggles are not resolved through your vow. Deliverance comes from walking in self control.

Single:

What is your weaknesses as it relates to dying to your flesh?

_____

_____

_____

_____

_____

_____

_____

Wife:

What areas of the flesh do you and your husband struggle?
Do you deal with these issues by exposing them or covering them?
Ask the Holy Spirit to give you wisdom on handling these areas of your marriage.

_____

_____

_____

_____

_____

_____

_____

Day 14

Submission

Sub- Support The Mission of your marriage or support the mission of Jesus Christ. Submission is just staying on one accord and in agreement for the vision, goals & plans for God, your marriage, family & personal goals.

Meditation:
Living life without being submitted to God will lead you to much heartache & disappointment. Without everyone being in their rightful position, the family will fall apart.

The structure of the family is the Husband who is submitted to God, The Wife Who is Submitted to her husband, the husband and wife Submitted to each other and the children following.

If you build your marriage on the right foundation and stay submitted, God will support and strengthen the weak areas of your marriage. When you get out of position, you leave room for the devil to destroy your marriage.

Single:

Submit to God, resist the devil and he will flee. God is leading you to your husband so he can find you. Are you fully submitted to God?

_____

_____

_____

_____

_____

_____

Wives:

Even if your husband is not submitted to God, stay in position and seek God for wisdom and guidance and will experience victory. What areas do you struggle to submit to your husband?

_____

_____

_____

_____

_____

Single Wife Prayer:
Dear Lord,
Thank You for grace for my Season of preparation. Teach me to die to my flesh and help me to operate in self control. Expose and reveal the root of my issue and give me the truth that will set me free. Help me to submit to you & resist the devil. I know you are teaching me the structure of a marriage. Strengthen me as I submit to your process and grow in my relationship with you so I can be ready for my husband.
In Jesus Name Amen

Wife Prayer:
Dear Lord,
Teach me the Power Of Submission so that I keep my house in order. Lead and guide my husband and I will follow him as he follows you. Help my children to follow us and not get caught up in the world. Let our family flow and build our lives on your strong foundation and the gates of hell cannot prevail against us. Thank you for helping me to cover the multitude of sins in my marriage. Help me die to my flesh and not satisfy anything hidden within me that is lustful.
In Jesus Name Amen

_____

_____

_____

_____

Make Your Request:

_____

_____

_____

_____

_____

_____

Notes:

_____

_____

_____

_____

_____

_____

_____

Day 15

Effective Communication

Meditation:
James 1:19 My dear brothers and sisters, take note of this:
Everyone should be quick to listen, slow to speak and slow to
become angry.

Examination:
Communication is a major key component to every relationship in your life. Oftentimes miscommunication is the root
cause to a relationship that falls.

Communicating with God not only requires you to talk to
God, it also requires you to listen.
- Talk to God.
- Make your requests.
- Thank Him for it.
- Meditate on Gods word.
- Listen for his instructions.

The key to communicating with God is not in talking to him,
it's listening to his voice to receive his instructions.

If you're frustrated about being misunderstood, Invite the Holy Spirit Into the conversation so he can be the mediator. Effective Communication requires you to discern Timing, Tact & Tone.

- Listen to understand
- Seek the Holy Spirit to get wisdom and instructions concerning your situation.
- Say what you need to say at the right time.
- Speak in a way that your words are honey to their ears.
- Peacemakers are blessed so keep the peace so God can give you Breakthrough in your relationships.

Single:
What are you confused about in your single season?
Ask God the right questions and listen for his answer.

_____

_____

_____

_____

_____

_____

_____

Wife:

What are you frustrated about concerning your life or marriage?

_____

_____

_____

_____

_____

_____

_____

Single/Wife Prayer:

Dear Lord,

Train my ear to hear your voice and obey your instructions. Help me to develop effective communication in all of my relationships. If I am at fault in hurting anyone with my words or because of dysfunctional communication forgive me.

Teach me to listen to understand and receive the truth that sets me free.

In Jesus Name Amen

Make Your Request:

_____

_____

_____

_____

_____

Notes:

_____

_____

_____

_____

_____

_____

_____

Day 16

Financial Frustration

Finances is one of the major causes of divorce. Not being a good steward of your finances and doing things out of order will create so much stress in your life. You have to develop an intimate relationship with money. God desires for you to prosper as long as you follow Kingdom Principles.

Meditation:
1 Timothy 6:10 For the love of money is the root of all kinds of evil. By craving it, some have wandered away
from the faith and pierced themselves with many sorrows.

Examination:
It doesn't matter how bad your finances are, when you live by Kingdom principles and not have a love for money

Steps To Manifest Financial Breakthrough:
- Give God the Tithe- 1st 10% of your Income, each paycheck or business transaction and he promises to open the windows of heaven, pour you out a blessing that you have no room to receive.
- Give your Offering
- Be a cheerful giver
- Give the poor

- Live your life on a budget
- Stay on one accord & in agreement with your spouse concerning finances.
- Resist compulsive spending
- Pay your bills on time
- Pay your taxes
- Speak to your mountain of debt.
- Expect supernatural blessings to overtake your finances.

Get Your Finances In Order:

_____

_____

_____

_____

_____

_____

_____

_____

_____

_____

_____

_____

Single Wife Prayer:
Dear Lord,
Forgive me if I have any love for money. Help me to put you 1st concerning my finances and be a good steward over all that you've blessed me with. I renounce the spirit of debt and poverty in my life. I cancel any bloodline curse over my finances. I will create a Dynasty that will manifest Generational blessings.
In Jesus Name Amen

Wife Prayer:
Dear Lord,
Forgive me if I have any love for money. Help me to put you 1st concerning my finances and be a good steward over all that you've blessed me with. I renounce the spirit of debt and poverty in my life. I cancel any bloodline curse over my finances. I will create a Dynasty that will manifest Generational blessings. Help my husband and I to stay on one accord toward our spending. I cancel the root of divorce being caused by us not being a good steward over all that you have blessed us with.
In Jesus Name Amen

Areas That You Have A Love For Money:

_____

_____

_____

_____

_____

Make Your Request:

_____

_____

_____

_____

_____

_____

Notes:

_____

_____

_____

_____

_____

_____

Day 17

Kingdom Family

Cover your house and bloodline in prayer. Leave no room for the devil as he causes conflicts, dissensions, drama and confusion. Be the peacemaker for your family and don't allow the enemy to separate & divide your home.

The dysfunction of your family can be covered in Gods love. Ask the Holy Spirit For Wisdom and guidance as it relates to defeating the enemy. If you Fight in the flesh it will become a bloody mess.

Ways to defeat the enemy:
- Put on the full armor of God.
- The fight is fixed and you've already won.
- The weapons of your warfare are not carnal but mighty in God By the pulling down of strongholds.
- Love covers a multitude of sins.
- Give your loved ones the same grace & mercy that God gives you.
- Blessed are peacemakers, they are true Daughters Of God.
- You are going to Win your family by faith through Gods love.

What area do you need God to deliver your family?

Say It With Me: Everything Attached To Me Wins.

_____

_____

_____

_____

_____

_____

_____

Single/Wife Prayer:
Dear Lord,
Cover my family in the blood of Jesus. No weapons formed against us shall prosper. Any tongue that rise against us shall be destroyed. Teach us to love one another like you. Give us wisdom and guidance to handle offense, hurt, shame and pain. Let their be deliverance from every shackle that the enemy has set up against you. Thank you for restoring my family and strengthening us to walk in unity, peace, joy and happiness.
In Jesus Name Amen

Make Your Request:

_____

_____

_____

_____

_____

Notes:

_____

_____

_____

_____

_____

_____

Day 18

Kingdom Children

Meditation:
Proverbs 22:6 Train up a child in the way he should go, even when he is old he will not depart from it.

Examination:
For those who are married and desire children but have not been able to conceive, anoint your womb everyday and say "Anointed to be a Mother" stand on Psalms 37:3-5

My Children Call Me Blessed
Train your children up in the word of God. Teach them to fall in love with Jesus and not fall in love with the things of this world.

- Keep them involved in Church activities so they can learn to seek 1st The Kingdom Of God and live a righteous lifestyle.
- Teach them to honor their mother and father and respect God.
- Teach them to Walk by faith and not by sight.
- Teach them to treat their body as a temple.

- Teach them to respect those in authority.
- Teach them to walk in Kingdom Authority as King & Queen.
- Help them to fulfill their Purpose.
- Help them to walk out their Destiny.

What areas do you need God to move concerning your children?

Single/Wife Prayer:
Dear Lord,
Help me to train up my children in your word. Deliver them from any rebellion and dishonor. Teach them to walk in your ways and precepts. Give them discernment to make wise decisions and choose those around them wisely. Expose, reveal and remove any person, place or thing that you never authorized to be in their life. They hear your voice and obey your instructions & the voice of a stranger they will never follow. In Jesus Name Amen

_____

_____

_____

_____

_____

_____

Day 19

Fight For Your Family

It is so important that you recognize who you are fighting against. The enemies job is to kill, steal and destroy families. He knows that families that stay together, pray together and stand on the word together, have the power to tear down the kingdom of darkness. You truly need to understand who you are really fighting against. You have already won the fight before you get in the ring when you become doers of the word.

We are in a season that we need to train ourselves to win through the word of God. The word of God has the answer to any question and it has the solution to any problem. You have to fight for your family so you can see the results of what your'e praying for.

Meditation:
Ephesians 6:12 For we are not fighting against flesh-and-blood enemies, but against evil rulers and authorities of the unseen world, against mighty powers in this dark world, and against evil spirits in the heavenly places.

Examination:

Most families are struggling because of conflict, mis-communication and dysfunction. Let us walk through the word to see what God says about the problems you may be having in your family. This is not the time to give up on your loved ones. This is the time for you to have faith in the word of God and see the results of all of his promises come to life in your family. Don't allow your struggles and frustrations to take over your life. God is the same yesterday, today and forever more.

What areas is your family struggling?

_____

_____

_____

_____

_____

Single/Wife Prayer:

Dear Lord,

Cover my family in the blood of Jesus. No weapons formed against us shall prosper, any tongue that rise against us shall be destroyed. Destroy every generational curse and pull down every stronghold. We shall be satisfied with a peaceful, loving life filled with Gods grace, mercy and his unconditional love.

In Jesus Name Amen

Day 20

Gods Favor

Meditation:

Proverbs 12:4 A worthy wife is a **crown** for **her husband**, but a disgraceful woman is like cancer in his bones.

Examination:

You are the favor crown of God and your husband. It requires you to be a good thing so your crown can shine and God can get the glory from your story. There are things that can disgrace God or your husband. Disrespect, dishonor, attitude problems, cutting words, jealousy, sin or living outside of the character of Christ are some of the major ways to disgrace God or your husband. God wants you walk worthy of your crown as a Queen in the Kingdom.

What are ways that you miss walking in Gods favor because of your disgrace?

_____

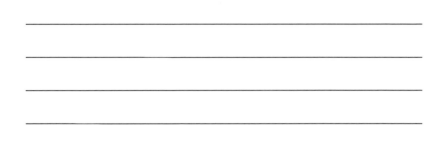

Single Wife Prayer:

Dear Lord,

Forgive me for any disgrace that I have carried toward you. Help me to change the areas of my life where I don't exemplify Queen Etiquette. I desire to live a life that is pleasing to you as my shine brings you glory.

In Jesus Name Amen

Wife Prayer:

Dear Lord,

Forgive me for any disgrace that I may have caused my husband. Help me in the areas of my weakness so I can be his good thing and my wife crown can glorify you. Let my crown bling with Gems that represent me overcoming the struggles in our marriage. Teach my husband to live a life that is pleasing in your eyes. Help him to see and appreciate me as the Queen that you have called me to be.

In Jesus Name Amen

Day 21

Be Quiet

A Winning Wife is a quiet and meek wife who knows how to be silent in the natural and be loud in the spirit. The enemy fears a woman that knows that she is a Queen that has the power to decree a thing and it be established. As wives we can complain, nag and talk too much as God is working behind the scenes of our lives.

Single women complain about being single and wives complain about not being content in their marriage. God told us in his word that we win we are quiet and meek. I will never forget when God taught me that if I would be quiet, the Holy Spirit would speak on my behalf. That lesson was life changing and I'm learning to master being quiet and meek.

Meditation:

1 Peter 3:1 Wives, in the same way submit yourselves to your own husbands so that, if any of them do not believe the word, they may be won over without words by the behavior of their wives.

Examination:

Single: Becoming wife material is attained by a quiet and meek spirit. Your single season is teaching you to be content as you become one with God and yourself. If your'e moaning and complaining about being alone, you are losing and that may be what's holding up your husband from finding you.

What are your complaints to God? Do you think that your complaints have hindered you from embracing this season and evolving into a Winning Wife?

_____

_____

_____

_____

_____

Wife: No matter if your husband is positioned to lead or not, God gave you a formula to win him over with a quiet and meek spirit. Are you complaining to your husband and God or have you taken your authority to make a decree over your marriage?

_____

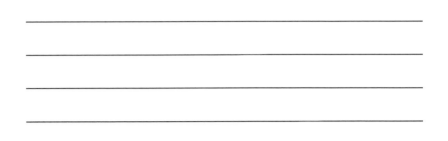

Single Wife Prayer:

Dear Lord,

Forgive me for complaining about being alone when you are preparing me to be a winning wife. Help me to embrace my process to my evolution as I learn to become a winning wife. Anything in me that is not pleasing in my sight, expose, reveal and remove it so I can be all that you need me to be.

In Jesus Name Amen

Wife Prayer:

Dear Lord,

Forgive me for failing at being a quiet and meek wife. Help me to watch my words and deliver me from complaining about my husband needing to change. Use me as an example of your love, grace and mercy to my husband. Help him to lead our family and make it exciting for me to follow. Strengthen our marriage and cover our flaws and issues in the blood of Jesus. No weapons formed against us shall prosper. Any tongue that rise against us shall be destroyed.

In Jesus Name Amen

Make Your Request:

_____

_____

_____

_____

_____

_____

Notes:

_____

_____

_____

_____

_____

_____

_____

Made in the USA
Lexington, KY
16 February 2018